D1558545

Discover Greece

Richard Spilsbury

PowerKiDS
press.

New York

Published in 2012 by the Rosen Publishing Group, Inc.
29 East 21st Street, New York, NY 10010

Copyright © 2012 Wayland/The Rosen Publishing Group, Inc.

First Edition

Concept Design: Jason Billin
Editor: Jennifer Sanderson
Designer: Amy Sparks
Picture Research: Amy Sparks, Jennifer Sanderson
Consultant: Elaine Jackson

Photographs:
Cover, WTPix/Steve White-Thomson; 1, Shutterstock/Mikael Damkier; 3 (bottom), Shutterstock/Rechitan Sorin, (top), Shutterstock/Ollirg; 4 (map), Stefan Chabluk; 5, Shutterstock/Drabovich Olga; 6, Shutterstock/Mikael Damkier; 7, Shutterstock/Piotr Tomicki; 8, Shutterstock/ Insuratelu Gabriela Gianina; 9, Shutterstock/ompuinfoto; 10, Shutterstock/Rechitan Sorin; 11, Getty Images/Louisa Gouliamaki/Stringer; 12, Alamy/Terry Harris; 13, Alamy; 14, Photolibrary/Superstock; 15, Photolibrary/Philip Enticknap/The Travel Library; 16, Alamy/Terry Harris; 17, Alamy/Asistidis Vafeiadakis; 18, Getty Images/Fayez Nureldine; 19, Shutterstock/Albert Barr; 20, WTPix/Steve White-Thomson; 21, Shutterstock/Steve Rosset; 22, Shutterstock/Mordeccy; 23, Shutterstock/Paul Cowan; 24, WTPix/Steve White-Thomson; 25, Shutterstock/Ollirg; 26, Dreamstime/Patrimonio; 27, Shutterstock/Dr. Le Thanh Hung; 28, Dreamstime/Irakite; 29, Shutterstock/Mihai Dancaescu.

Library of Congress Cataloging-in-Publication Data

Spilsbury, Richard, 1963–
Discover Greece / by Richard Spilsbury. — 1st ed.
    p. cm. — (Discover countries)
Includes index.
ISBN 978-1-4488-6622-9 (library binding) — ISBN 978-1-4488-7048-6 (pbk.) —
ISBN 978-1-4488-7049-3 (6-pack)
1. Greece—Juvenile literature. I. Title.
DF717.S69 2012
949.5–dc23

2011029060

Manufactured in Malaysia

CPSIA Compliance Information: Batch #WW2102PK: For Further Information contact Rosen Publishing, New York, New York at 1-800-237-9932

Contents

Discovering Greece

The Greek mainland juts out into the Mediterranean Sea and is surrounded by thousands of islands. Greece is internationally renowned as a tourist destination, not only for its natural beauty, but also for its fascinating heritage.

A Changing Country

Athens is the capital of Greece. It has been an important city for thousands of years. It was the center of civilization where theater, literature, and democracy developed. In the following centuries, the country changed massively. It was occupied by Ottoman Turks and achieved independence from the Ottoman Empire only in 1829.

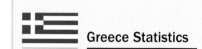

Greece Statistics

Area: 50, 949 sq. miles (131,957 sq. km)
Capital City: Athens
Government Type: Parliamentary Republic
Bordering Countries: Albania, Bulgaria, Turkey, Macedonia
Currency: Euro (€)
Language: Greek 99% (official), other 1%

Greece is a European country that is about the same size as Louisiana. The country shares borders with Albania, Bulgaria, Turkey, and Macedonia.

During World War II, hundreds of thousands of Greeks died when their country was occupied by German, Italian, and Bulgarian forces. After the war, the economy collapsed and Greece suffered further during a brutal civil war, which left the country politically unstable. In 1967, a group of military officers seized power and soon ended the rule of the Greek royal family.

Modern Greece

In 1975, a new era began when Greece became a democratic republic. Political stability in the country allowed the economy to grow, especially under Prime Minister Andreas Papandreou, who was in power during much of the 1980s and again in the mid-1990s. Tourism and the shipping industry grew. In 1981, Greece joined the European Union (EU). In 2001, it adopted the euro as its currency.

A Country in Crisis

Following the global economic crisis of 2008, and a period of borrowing money from banks, Greece could not repay its debts, which had risen to $400 billion. European countries agreed to repay part of the debt if Greece reduced its spending. The government announced many austerity measures, which included cutting jobs and public services, raising taxes, and plans to sell some small Greek islands. The effects of the economic crisis will define Greece for years to come.

● The Acropolis is one of Greece's most famous ancient buildings. In 2010, it was the site of public protests against the spending cuts made by the government in response to the economic crisis.

DID YOU KNOW?

The first Olympic Games took place in ancient Greece in about 776 BCE. During the Games, war with other states and empires was banned.

Landscape and Climate

Greece's 2,000 or so islands make up one-fifth of its total area and the country has a long, beautiful coastline. Inland Greece is dominated by high mountains.

Geography

The large Pindus mountain range extends from the northwest to the southeast on the mainland and is often called the spine of Greece. Mount Olympus is Greece's highest peak. Greece is situated in a region that has many fault lines and these can cause earthquakes and volcanoes. Some islands, such as Santorini, were formed by volcanoes that erupted in the past. Less than 20 percent of the Greek landscape is lowland, with river valleys and basins created by lakes in the past. Only 170 of Greece's islands are inhabited. Crete is the largest of these.

Facts at a Glance

Land Area: 50,443 sq. miles (130,647 sq. km)

Highest Point: Mount Olympus 9,570 feet (2,917 m)

Coastline: 8,498 miles (13,676 km)

Longest River: Aliakmonos River 185 miles (297 km)

Santorini is made up of a large semicircular island next to several smaller ones. They are the remaining pieces of a giant volcano that erupted more than 3,000 years ago.

◄ Mount Olympus,
in northern Greece,
is made up of 52
rocky peaks with
steep wooded slopes.

Climate

Greece has a typical Mediterranean climate.
In summer, it is warm or hot across the country
and there is little or no rain. In winter, it is
generally mild. There can be spells of very cold
weather and it can snow, though this happens
mostly in the mountain regions and rarely on
the islands. Winter is the wettest season.
Spring and autumn are short seasons when
the weather can be very changeable. The
amount of sunshine varies from 4 to 5 hours a
day in the middle of the winter to as many as
14 hours a day in the middle of the summer.

Extreme Heat

There are sometimes heatwaves in inland
Greece during the summer. During a heatwave,
temperatures can reach above 100 °F (38 °C)
for a day or more. Heatwaves can cause
heatstroke, which may result in headaches,
dizziness, and even death. During a heatwave,
people use a lot of power to run air-conditioning
systems. This can cause power shortages. The
intense heat and lack of rain can also cause
widespread forest fires and water shortages.

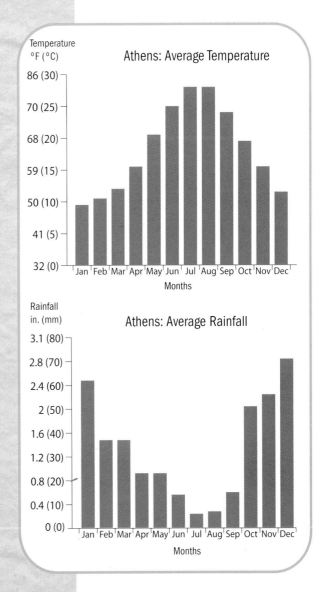

Population and Health

The Greek population is shrinking. One-fifth of Greeks are older than 65, and the birth rate is lower than the death rate. However, this may change in the future, depending on migration rates and the effectiveness of the healthcare system.

Population

Most of the population are ethnic Greeks, but there are some smaller ethnic groups living in the country. These include Macedonians, Albanians, and Turks, some of whose ancestors became Greek citizens following border disputes between Greece and its neighboring countries. They also include Roma, commonly known as Tsingani, who move around the country during the year.

Migration

The biggest cause of migration in Greece is its economy. In the late nineteenth century, about one-sixth of the Greek population emigrated to the USA and Egypt when the price of currants, the major agricultural export, fell. After World War II, there was a second wave of economic emigration to countries such as Germany and Australia.

▶ The ethnic mix in Greece is gradually changing through immigration. These African immigrants are selling goods on the streets of Athens.

Facts at a Glance

Total Population: 11.1 million
Life Expectancy at Birth: 80 years
Children Dying Before the Age of Five: 0.6%

Today 5 million Greeks live overseas, sometimes grouped in particular cities. For example, in Australia, Melbourne's Greek population is bigger than that in all but seven Greek cities. In recent decades, there has been immigration of different peoples into Greece, many from poorer neighboring countries, such as Albania and Romania, but also from war-torn Afghanistan.

Health

Since 1983, the Greek National Health Service has provided free or low-cost healthcare for its tax-paying residents. However, as most hospitals and doctors' offices are concentrated in cities, access to healthcare in rural areas is more limited. The World Health Organization ranks the Greek healthcare system higher than those of the UK and USA. This is based on factors such as longer lifespans and lower infant mortality. Today, Greece has the highest obesity rate in Europe and this, along with reduced health spending owing to economic problems, will put pressure on the healthcare system.

DID YOU KNOW?
Greece has a network of special SOS doctors who visit patients' homes to deal with health emergencies. SOS doctors are independent of hospitals and clinics but the government pays for the service.

🔺 This woman from Xenia, in Crete, is 100 years old. Many people say that the traditional Greek diet of fresh vegetables, fish, and olive oil contributes to long lifespans.

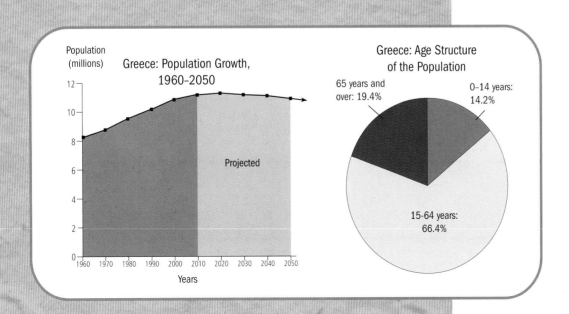

Greece: Population Growth, 1960–2050

Population (millions)

Projected

Years

Greece: Age Structure of the Population

65 years and over: 19.4%

0–14 years: 14.2%

15-64 years: 66.4%

Settlements and Living

Most Greeks live in apartments, rather than private houses. The apartment buildings are mostly in coastal cities where people can find work.

Homes

Most apartment buildings are several stories high and were built in the first half of the twentieth century. At this time, cities expanded to accommodate the growing number of people moving from rural villages in order to find work. Today, homes are generally owned not rented, and a typical village home has room for one family. People living in cities may also keep village homes, especially on the coast, which their families use for vacations.

◉ Some of the most remarkable settlements in Greece are the monasteries that are perched high on steep mountains in Meteora, which means "supsended in air."

Facts at a Glance

Urban Population:
6.8 million

Rural Population:
4.3 million

Population of Largest City:
3.2 million (Athens)

DID YOU KNOW?
Ancient Greek houses were often built around open courtyards where people cooked and children played, and where women could spend time outside. Inside there were separate living areas for men and women.

Settlement Patterns

In the past, the Greek population was more spread out and many people lived inland in villages, often isolated in the mountains. Today, two-thirds of the Greek population is concentrated in cities. The capital, Athens, is the country's most populous city. Athens became important as an ancient trading center between Greece and countries around the Aegean and Mediterranean seas. Many of the biggest cities in Greece, including Thessaloniki, are on the coast and have grown because they have good natural harbors for shipping.

Population in Urban Area (%)

Greek Population: Rural/Urban Split, 1960–2050

Projected

Years

Illegal Immigrants

Greece has the highest number of illegal immigrants in Europe. They concentrate near ports with the hope of finding work or travelling to Western European countries, such as Italy, to earn a better living. As a result of this migration, large slums have developed near the ports of Athens and Patras. Slums are a problem because they take over land and put unplanned pressure on resources, such as water and electricity. The Greek government has tried to reduce the slum problem and force people to return to their own countries by knocking down buildings and detaining the illegal immigrants in special camps.

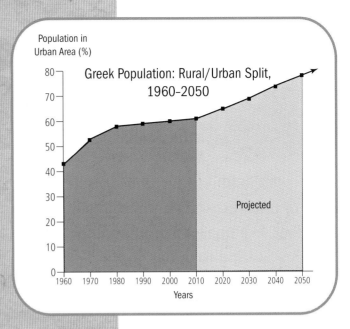

⬩ The conditions in this Patras slum were so poor that the Greek government moved the immigrants who lived there into military barracks. Immigrants choose Patras because ferries cross from the port to Italy.

Family Life

Family life is important in Greece and families take care of each other. Different generations often work together, live near each other, and spend a lot of time socializing together, too.

Greek Families

In the past, men tended to go out to work and women stayed at home. Fathers were the dominant members of the household. This officially changed in 1983 with a Family Law Act that gave Greek women equality. Today, many women go out to work, but in some homes the father is still the head of the family while the women do the majority of the cooking and housework. Most young adults continue to live with their parents until they marry. Elderly parents usually live with one of their adult children.

▶ Greek grandparents often have a close bond with their grandchildren because they live in shared family homes.

Marriage

Most people in Greece marry when they are in their late 20s to mid-30s. Wedding ceremonies are usually held in a church and are followed by lavish meals, music, and dancing. Instead of giving gifts, guests often pin or tape money to the bride's dress. Greece has a very low divorce rate compared to other countries in Europe. This is thought to be a result of the importance of families being close and spending time together in Greek culture.

Children

Today, most Greek couples have one or two children. As most Greeks are religious (see pages 14–15), their babies are baptized 40 days to a year after they are born. At this ceremony, babies are officially given a name, which is almost always a saint's name. Both parents are usually involved in bringing up their children and children also spend a lot of time with members of their extended family, including grandparents, aunts, and uncles.

(see pages 14–15)

▶ A Greek Orthodox priest in Trikala baptizes a baby by anointing it with holy water and oils.

Religion and Beliefs

Greece is a religious country and almost the whole population (98 percent) follows the Greek Orthodox faith. The Greek constitution guarantees its citizens freedom of religion, and there are other religious groups, too, the next largest of which is Muslims.

The Greek Orthodox Church

Orthodox Christians share many of the same beliefs as other Christians, but differ in the way they worship. A distinctive feature of the Orthodox churches is their grand services, which about a quarter of the population attends each week. Many more people go to the big annual services. Greek Orthodox churches are full of religious icons, which worshipers honor with candles. Many people have icons in their homes, too.

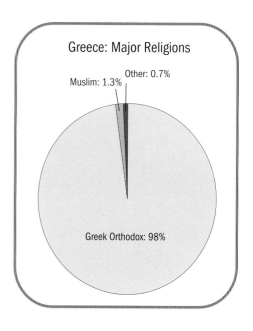

Greece: Major Religions

Muslim: 1.3%
Other: 0.7%
Greek Orthodox: 98%

Men train to become Greek Orthodox priests at special religious colleges called seminaries. Women cannot become priests, but can live as nuns.

Church Power in Greece

The Orthodox Church has a lot of influence on Greek society. For example, all children have to study religion at school and they pray together before starting lessons in the mornings. The Church also puts pressure on the government to take decisions that fit with its principles, such as banning gay marriages. The Church is the country's largest and wealthiest landowner. It plans to build wind farms on some of its land to make renewable energy that it can sell to the country's electricity suppliers.

Festivals and Celebrations

Most of the major festivals and celebrations in Greece are religious. Almost everyone celebrates Christmas. On Christmas Eve, families bake large, sweet loaves called *Christopsomo*, or "Christ-bread." Most people spend Easter in their native villages. As well as church services, there are candlelit processions on Good Friday, fireworks at midnight on Saturday, and a feast of roast lamb on Easter Sunday. In Greece, people also have parties on their name days. These are the saint's days of the saints with whom people share their names.

▶ At Easter, the most sacred celebration in the Greek Orthodox faith, people set their tables with baskets of red eggs to symbolize the blood of Christ.

DID YOU KNOW?
Some Greeks carry a blue charm with an eye painted on it to ward off "the evil eye," a form of bad luck that someone can pass to you when they look on you with envy.

Education and Learning

Education in ancient Greece was mostly for boys. It varied, depending on where people lived. For example, in Sparta, young boys were sent to military camps to learn survival and military skills. In Athens, boys usually learned reading, writing, math, wrestling, and how to play the lyre.

Schools in Greece

Today, the Greek government provides free education for all children. School is compulsory, or required, from the age of 6 until 15. The subjects studied include history, math, physical education, religion, geography, science, and languages. After compulsory school, most young Greeks spend three years at either Eniaia Lykeia (EL) colleges, where they prepare to go to universities, or Technical Vocational Educational schools (TEEs), where they study trades, from boat engineering to hotel management.

Facts at a Glance

Children in Primary School:
Male 100%, Female 99%

Children in Secondary School:
Male 92%, Female 93%

Literacy Rate (Over 15 Years):
96%

⬤ In ancient Greek times, girls in many parts of the country were not allowed to go to school. Today, young Greeks of both sexes go to school.

Language Studies

The Greek language has existed since the fourteenth century BCE. By the eighteenth century, it had more than 600,000 words. Some words came from ancient Greek and some came from languages spoken during the country's occupation by the Roman and Ottoman Empires. In the 1830s, a new official version of Greek, called *Katharevousa*, was created. It was based on ancient Greek. Although Katharevousa was taught in schools and used in books and newspapers, most Greeks spoke a simpler modern Greek, called Demotic, which finally became official in 1976. Today, Greek children speak Demotic but they also learn some ancient Greek during cultural studies. English is also taught, since it is useful for jobs in tourism.

Greek Roma

Most Roma children living in Greece are poorly educated. This is because their families speak Romani at home, so they get little support in learning Greek. They change schools as their families move around, too. They also often get married very young and start to work without completing their schooling. The Greek government is trying to improve Roma education by training language support teachers and encouraging enrollment in schools.

DID YOU KNOW?

During wartime, Greek law states that men as young as 17 years old can be called to serve in the army.

▼ Just as Spartan boys were taught military skills, today the government requires all Greek men between the ages of 18 and 45 to spend at least 12 months in the army.

Employment and Economy

Most Greeks work in the service industry, which includes government and private jobs. However, owing to its austerity measures (see page 5), unemployment is on the rise in Greece, especially among young people who lack work experience.

Jobs

The average wage in Greece is around two-thirds of the average across European countries that use the euro. Immigrants make up nearly one-fifth of the work force, mainly in agricultural and unskilled jobs.

Facts at a Glance

Contributions to GDP:
  Agriculture: 3%
  Industry: 21%
  Services: 76%
Labor Force:
  Agriculture: 12.4%
  Industry: 22.4%
  Services: 65.2%
Female Labor Force:
  40% of total
Unemployment Rate: 9.5%

▼ The construction of stadiums and other infrastructure projects before the 2004 Olympics boosted the Greek economy but was financed by borrowing money from banks.

Many businesses are small and family-run, so some people take several jobs, for example working in fishing and renting kayaks to tourists. Women make up less than half of the workforce, but this is a higher proportion than in the past.

Economy

In the early twentieth century, farming, herding, seafaring, fishing, and traditional crafts were still at the heart of the Greek economy. The economy grew after World War II because of aid given by countries, such as Germany, to help repair damage and improve the infrastructure. It grew again after Greece started to use the euro because it could then borrow money more easily from banks. Today, 40 percent of the Greek gross domestic product (GDP) comes from public service jobs, including those in schools and government offices. The Greek economy also relies partly on payments from Greeks living overseas, for example in the USA or Australia, to family members in Greece.

Natural Resources

One reason that manufacturing industries contribute little to the Greek economy is that the country has few natural resources. Greece has supplies of bauxite (the rock from which the metal aluminium comes), stone (including marble), some oil, and lignite. Lignite is a type of coal used in most of Greece's power plants. It is more polluting to the atmosphere than other types of coal.

In summer, the arrival of tourists by ferry provides many Greek islanders with extra income. For example, some islanders rent out rooms.

DID YOU KNOW?
Marble from Thassos, an island in the Aegean, is world-renowned for its bright white color. It has been used since ancient times for building temples and monuments and for sculptures.

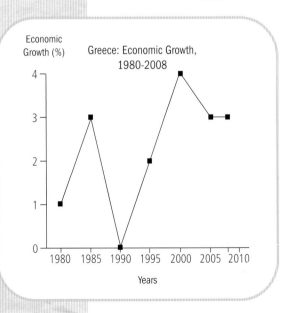

Economic Growth (%)

Greece: Economic Growth, 1980-2008

Industry and Trade

Tourism and shipping are the biggest industries in Greece, followed by manufacturing and construction. This explains why the value of imports into Greece is much smaller than that of exports.

Tourism and Shipping

Today, Greece attracts more visitors each year than its own population. Most visitors come from other parts of Europe, but increasingly people come from further afield, including China. The tourism industry varies in scale, from people who sell sunglasses and moped rental companies to hotel complexes and cruise ships. Overall, tourism contributes one-sixth of Greece's GDP and is found all over the country, particularly in Athens and the islands. However, the country faces competition from other Mediterranean destinations, including nearby Croatia and Turkey, which also attract vacationers.

DID YOU KNOW?
In the 1950s and 1960s, Greek shipping tycoons, including Stavros Niarchos and Aristotle Onassis, were some of the wealthiest men in the world.

The Tholos at the sanctuary of Athena Pronaia, in Delphi, is one of Greece's most popular tourist attractions.

The Greek shipping industry has one of the largest non-military fleets in the world. Most ships are large bulk carriers carrying cargoes between developing countries and Europe.

Other Industries

Manufacturing, or making things from raw materials, contributes about one-eighth of Greece's GDP. Factories are mostly located near Athens and make goods such as food and beverages, aluminium products, textiles, and chemicals. However, one of the world's largest cement factories is located at the port of Vólos, in northeast Greece, largely because the raw material limestone is quarried nearby. The construction industry builds not only public projects, such as airports, but also private houses and hotels. During the economic crisis of 2008, the construction industry in Greece shrank and many people lost their jobs.

Trading

Around two-fifths of Greece's trade is with other EU members, especially Germany and Italy. It exports mostly food products, including grapes, nuts, dried fruit, and olive oil. Other exports are clothing, machinery, and some refined fuels. Greece's major imports are chemicals, ship and boat engines, crude oil, and vehicles, such as cars and trucks.

⚫ Greek owners control one-fifth of all tankers in the world. The Greek shipping industry is thriving partly because of the demand for raw materials from growing Asian economies.

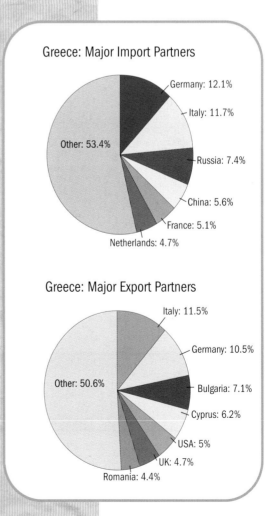

Greece: Major Import Partners

- Germany: 12.1%
- Italy: 11.7%
- Russia: 7.4%
- China: 5.6%
- France: 5.1%
- Netherlands: 4.7%
- Other: 53.4%

Greece: Major Export Partners

- Italy: 11.5%
- Germany: 10.5%
- Bulgaria: 7.1%
- Cyprus: 6.2%
- USA: 5%
- UK: 4.7%
- Romania: 4.4%
- Other: 50.6%

Farming and Food

Farming is a challenge in many parts of Greece, mainly because of the poor soils and lack of rain. Less than a third of the land in Greece's lowlands is used for growing crops. The rest is used for pasture or left as scrub and forest.

Agriculture

On the plains of Greece, farmers are able to grow corn, wheat, and cotton in huge fields. There are giant greenhouses where farmers grow crops, such as peppers and tomatoes, for export in winter. The country produces more black olives and high-quality olive oil than anywhere else in Europe.

Facts at a Glance

Farmland:
36% of total land area

Main Agricultural Exports:
Prepared fruit, olive oil, olives, tobacco

Main Agricultural Imports:
Cheese, beef, alcoholic drinks, pork, wheat

Average Daily Calorie Intake:
3,700

▼ Olive plantations are found across Greece, especially in the Kalamata region. There are around 120 million olive trees in the country. That is about 12 for each Greek citizen.

Farmers also grow grapes, which are sold fresh or dried, or made into wine. Livestock farmers keep mainly sheep and goats as these animals graze on arid land. Some also raise cattle, chickens, and pigs.

Fishing

Fishing has always been important to the Greek economy and diet. At sea, fishermen catch anchovies, sardines, mussels, tuna, octopus, lobster, and other seafood. There are also many fish farms along the coastline, and it is from these farms that fish is exported. Greece produces sea bass and sea bream.

Greek Food

The Greek diet was traditionally rich in fresh vegetables, fruit, olives, olive oil, bread, cheese, fish, and other seafood, with meat a rare luxury. These foods still form the main part of the country's diet, but people also eat more meat and processed food today. Some typical Greek foods are *taramasalata* (smoked cod eggs), *moussaka* (a baked dish with eggplant and tomatoes), and *baklava* (a sweet pastry filled with chopped nuts and syrup or honey).

⚫ Tavernas along the coast serve meals to tourists and locals. Fresh fish and other seafood, such as the lobster shown here, are some of the most popular items on the menu.

DID YOU KNOW?
On average, Greeks eat around 55 pounds (25 kg) of cheese per person each year. This is more than people of any other nationality eat. About half of this is feta, a white, salty cheese eaten with bread, in pastries, and in salad.

Transportation and Communications

It was only in the latter part of the twentieth century that all Greece's villages got electricity and roads. It has been a challenge to provide transportation and communications to the whole of the country because it has so many islands and mountains.

Water Transportation

Greek islands rely on regular ferry service to bring in goods and tourists. These ferries link not only mainland Greece with the islands, but also Greece with Italy. Inland, there are no navigable rivers. The Corinth Canal was built in the late 1800s to shorten trade routes from Italy to Athens. However, its shallow depth and narrow width mean many of today's modern ships cannot get through.

Facts at a Glance

Total Roads: 73,032 miles (117,533 km)

Paved Roads: 67,043 miles (107,895 km)

Major Airports: 20

Major Ports: 5

DID YOU KNOW?
On hilly islands with very steep, narrow roads, donkeys are still used for transporting goods from ports up to homes and businesses.

▼ Fast-moving hydrofoils, like this one, are a popular means of transportation, particularly for people travelling between islands.

Air and Rail

The main airport in Athens is linked to airports around the country, often near popular tourist destinations, such as Rhodes, but also close to major cities, including Alexandroupoli and Thessaloniki. In the mid-twentieth century, the only airline providing flights within Greece was Olympic Airlines, which was run by the government until 2009. Today, there are several airlines offering domestic flights. Although the Greek rail system is rather old, it is being updated. An important part of the improvement in transportation links is the construction of the Athens Metro, a subway which is designed to reduce traffic congestion in this busy city.

Communication

In Greece, around 5 million people use the Internet, which is less than half the population. There are around 2 million broadband connections in the country. Most Greeks find out news via radio or television, rather than on the Internet. A wide range of television and radio stations broadcast programs across the country. The number of cell phones is high, with almost every individual in the country owning one.

⚫ In 2004, the Rion-Antirion bridge was built to link the Peloponnese Peninsula to mainland Greece and shorten road journeys across the country. At 1.4 miles (2.25 km) long, it is the world's longest suspension bridge.

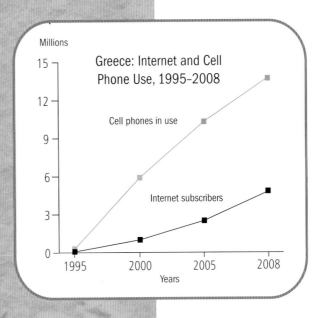

Millions

Greece: Internet and Cell Phone Use, 1995–2008

Cell phones in use

Internet subscribers

Years

Leisure and Tourism

When it is hot in summer, most Greeks spend their free time outdoors, socializing, eating, swimming, or fishing. In small towns and villages, it is traditional for people to walk up and down the main street or shore in the evening, meeting and greeting friends. This is called the *volta*.

Leisure and Sports

In the colder months, Greeks spend their leisure time at home watching television and gaming, going to the movies, or socializing in cafés. Playing sports is popular, too. The country's most popular sport is soccer, although basketball is also very popular. Other sports people enjoy include water polo, sailing, gymnastics, and track and field. In mountain resorts, such as Pelion and Delphi, people also ski and hunt animals, such as wild boar.

The Greek basketball team (in white) was ranked fourth in the world in 2010. Basketball is a popular sport in schools, and many towns have outside courts.

Facts at a Glance

Tourist Arrivals (Millions)	
2000	10.1
2005	13.1
2006	14.8
2007	15.9

The Arts

Greece has a rich arts heritage. It is famous for its ancient literature, including poems such as Homer's *Odyssey* and plays such as Sophocles' *Oedipus the King*. Its sculptures and architecture are still admired today. Traditional Greek instruments, such as the bouzouki (a stringed instrument), clarinets, and lyres, are still used to play a type of Greek music called *laika*. Today, laika musicians may also use modern instruments, such as keyboards. Many Greek people listen to pop, rock, and Western classical music.

Tourism

There are several reasons why Greece is such a popular tourist destination. The country has World Heritage sites, such as Rhodes, Delphi, and the remarkable monasteries at Mount Athos. Tourists also come for the sunshine and clear seas. They take part in diving, spearfishing, boating, and other watersports. The sheltered, wide bay and summer winds at Vassiliki make it a major windsurfing destination. Tourists enjoy visiting the islands to see their distinct cultures and features, such as the windmills of Crete. There are also festivals at which Greek dramas are performed, as well as free concerts and open-air films in many parks.

The theater at Epidaurus was built in the fourth century BCE and can seat 15,000 people. The acoustics are so good that everyone in the theater can hear words spoken softly from the stage.

DID YOU KNOW?
Tourism is so important that there is a special section of the police force, called the tourism police, to sort out tourists' problems. Its officers are trained in foreign languages.

Environment and Wildlife

Greece has a variety of habitats, including forests, scrublands, mountains, and coasts. These habitats are home to a range of wildlife, including some which are endemic to Greece, such as the 600 types of wildflowers that are found nowhere else in the world.

Greek Biodiversity

Among the pine and chestnut trees of the northern mountain forests, people see wildcats, boar, roe deer, and many birds, including vultures and eagles. Some of southern Europe's last remaining wolves and brown bears are found in the Pindus Mountains. In lowland meadows and scrublands, there are many reptiles, including snakes, lizards, and tortoises, as well as bigger animals, such as wild goats and porcupines. Off the coasts, there are 250 species of fish, squid, and lobster, as well as bigger animals, such as dolphins and sea turtles.

Facts at a Glance

Proportion of Area Protected:
1.8%

Biodiversity (Known Species):
5,522

Threatened Species: 27

🔻 Rare kri-kri goats are found in Crete's mountains.

Threats

Some of Greece's wild habitats are under threat. This endangers the animals and plants that live there. Trees are cut down to clear land for farming or building, and are destroyed in forest fires. Land is damaged by overgrazing. Tourism can be a problem when large hotels and other facilities are built on the coast. Fresh water supplies are also degraded by overuse, especially on islands, where water is often used to fill swimming pools. At sea, pollution from coastal resorts, shipping, and overfishing are threatening many marine animals and plants. These include the Mediterranean monk seal, which is one of the world's most endangered marine mammals.

Protection

One-fifth of Greece's land is protected. This includes 17 national parks, including marine parks, two United Nations biosphere reserves, and wetlands that are internationally important. There are also some specific projects aimed at particular habitats or animals. For example, the World Wide Fund for Nature is buying areas around the beaches of Laganas Bay to prevent coastal development for tourism. These beaches are important nesting sites for the loggerhead turtle.

◯ Conservation volunteers in Greece protect loggerhead turtles. For example, they clean up nesting beaches and rescue turtles that were injured when they got trapped in fishing nets.

DID YOU KNOW?
The large Greek island of Crete is home to hundreds of endemic species, including many orchids, the Cretan spiny mouse, a shrew, a badger, and the kri-kri goat.

Glossary

austerity measures (aw-STER-ih-tee MEH-zherz) Steps governments take to improve their economies.

baptize (BAP-tyz) To sprinkle someone with or to immerse someone in water to show that person's acceptance into the Christian faith.

biosphere reserve (BY-oh-sfeer rih-ZURV) Land that has been set aside to protect the things living there.

civil war (SIH-vul WOR) A war between two sides within one country.

climate (KLY-mut) The kind of weather a certain place has.

constitution (kon-stih-TOO-shun) The basic rules by which a country or a state is governed.

democratic (deh-muh-KRA-tik) Having to do with a government that is run by the people who live under it.

emigrate (EH-mih-grayt) To leave one's country to settle in another.

endangered (in-DAYN-jerd) In danger of no longer existing.

export (ek-SPORT) To send something to another place to be sold.

endemic (en-DEH-mik) Coming from, and often found only in, a place.

ethnic group (ETH-nik GROOP) A group of people who have the same race, beliefs, practices, or language, or who belong to the same country.

extended family (ek-STEN-ded FAM-lee) Members of a family beyond the parents and children.

Good Friday (GUD FRY-day) Day that marks the day on which Christians believe Jesus Christ died.

hydrofoil (HY-druh-foy-ul) A boat with wing-like parts that raises it out of the water.

icon (EYE-kon) A picture or image that is godly.

immigration (in-muh-GRAY-shun) People moving to another country to live.

import (IM-port) A good brought from one country to another.

independence (in-dih-PEN-dents) Freedom from the control or support of other people.

infant mortality (IN-funt mor-TAH-luh-tee) The percentage of babies that die before their first birthday.

infrastructure (IN-fruh-struk-cher) Things, such as roads, hospitals, and power plants, that are important for the people in a place.

lyre (LYR) A musical instrument with strings that is like a harp.

monastery (MAH-nuh-ster-ee) A house where people who have taken vows of faith live and work.

monk (MUNK) A man who is a member of a religious order.

nun (NUN) A woman who is a member of a religious order.

overfishing (oh-ver-FISH-ing) Catching too many fish.

overgrazing (oh-ver-GRAYZ-ing) When animals eat too many of the plants in an area.

republic (rih-PUH-blik) A form of government in which the authority belongs to the people.

saint (SAYNT) A person considered holy by a religion.

Topic Web

Use this topic web to explore Greek themes
in different areas of study.

Internet Technology

Use the Internet to compare Greece's health data to that of other countries. Identify one data category that suggests that Greece has a healthcare problem and one that suggests the country can care well for its citizens' health.

Science

Greece is a country with 8,498 miles (13,676 km) of coastline. Many tourists go to Greece to enjoy the beaches. Find out more about the environmental impact of coastal tourism, concentrating on freshwater resources and pollution.

Math

The ancient Greek mathematicians Archimedes and Pythagoras are famous for solving mathematical problems. Find out what Archimedes' principle and Pythagoras' theorem are and how were they discovered.

Geography

Research different shipping routes from around the world. Do you think the Suez Canal, in Egypt, has been important for the growth of the Greek shipping industry?

Greece

History

Find out what you can about the origins of the Olympic Games in Greece. Why did they start, where did they happen, and what sports events were first included?

Design and Technology

Find a recipe for and create a traditional Greek salad. Make it look as attractive as you can and serve it with fresh bread. Evaluate the balance of ingredients in this meal. Is this a healthy dish?

English

Many English words have Greek roots. Find as many English words as you can that use these Greek roots: hydro-, chrono-, phono-, photo-, poly-, philo-, and arch-. Once you know the meanings of the roots, can you work out the meanings of the words?

Citizenship

"Democracy" comes from a Greek word and means government by the people and for the people. What do you know about democracy in your area? How do your local government officials address people's concerns?

Further Reading, Web Sites, and Index

Further Reading

Let's Visit Greece by Susie Brooks (PowerKids Press, 2010)
National Geographic Countries of the World: Greece by Jen Green (National Geographic Children's Books, 2009)
This Is Greece by Miroslav Sasek (Universe, 2009)

Web Sites

Due to the changing nature of Internet links, PowerKids Press has developed an online list of Web sites related to the subject of this book. This site is updated regularly. Please use this link to access the list: www.powerkidslinks.com/discovc/greece

Index

20 70